seagulls

my nature
sticker activity book

At the Seashore

Olivia Cosneau

 Translated by
Yolanda Stern Broad

PRINCETON ARCHITECTURAL PRESS, NEW YORK

Dunes are fragile.

Along some coasts, wind carries away sand from the beach, forming hills. These hills are called dunes, and they are home to hedgehogs, lizards, toads, and little white snails. People plant reeds to protect the dunes. Their roots hold the sand in place.

Stick some white snails on the stems of the reeds.

Draw some more reeds.

There are lots of animals living in the sand!

A tiny hole in the sand tells you there's a worm buried there. It might also be a shellfish, like a cockle or a razor clam. Cockles have rounded shells. Razor clams are long and flat. They are both bivalves: they have two shells.

 Stick some seashells here.   *Draw some more.*

Some shellfish attach themselves to rocks.

Limpets have a foot they use like a suction cup to fasten themselves to rocks. They are very hard to pull off! Periwinkles look like snails. When danger looms, they close their shells with a little cover called an operculum.

Stick some limpets and periwinkles on the rocks.

Color the seaweed.

Where is the crab hiding?

A crab has ten legs and moves sideways (it sidles). As it grows, it outgrows its shell and leaves it behind. Then it is all soft and hides under a rock until its new shell hardens. There are several species of crab. The biggest kind is the brown crab. Brown crabs are very slow moving.

Stick on the crab's missing body parts.

Color the other crabs, following the color code.

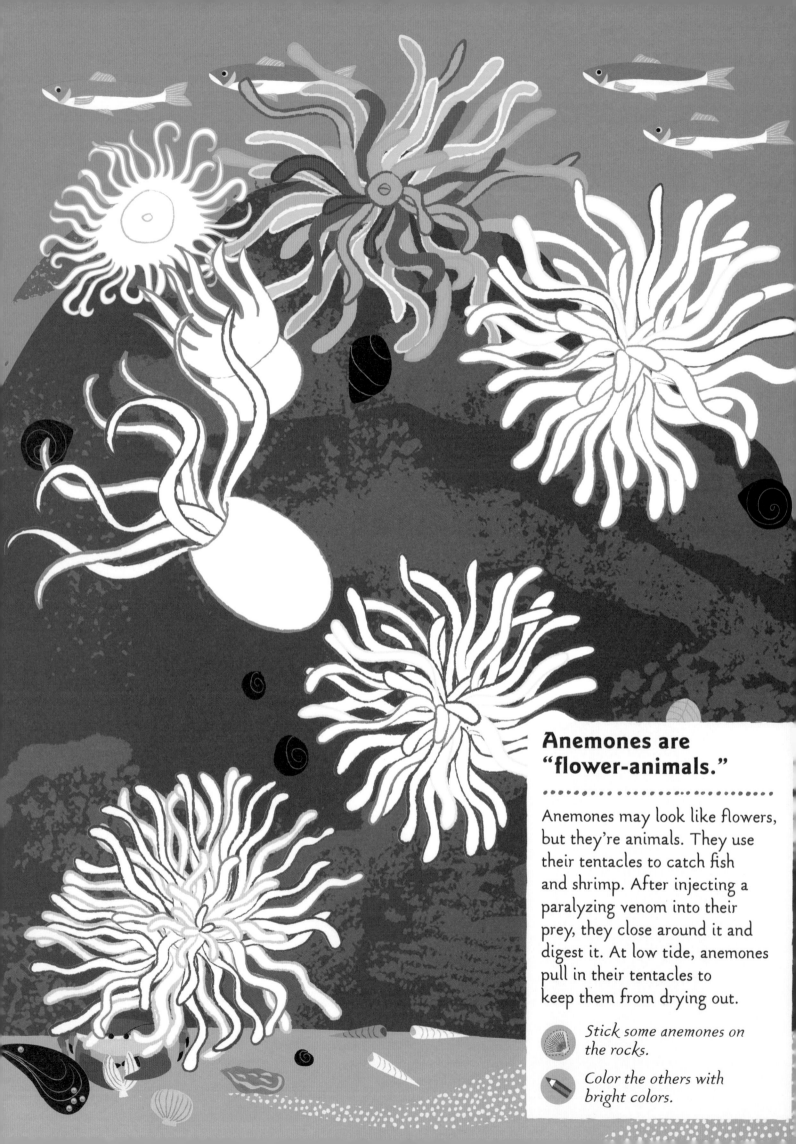

Anemones are "flower-animals."

Anemones may look like flowers, but they're animals. They use their tentacles to catch fish and shrimp. After injecting a paralyzing venom into their prey, they close around it and digest it. At low tide, anemones pull in their tentacles to keep them from drying out.

Stick some anemones on the rocks.

Color the others with bright colors.

Watch out for the jellyfish: it stings!

Jellyfish float along on the current. They move by expanding and contracting the bell-shaped upper part of their bodies. They have very elegant long tentacles and transparent, bluish bodies. But don't touch them: they sting!

Finish drawing and coloring the jellyfish.

Starfish don't have heads.

Starfish are powerful hunters of shellfish. They wrap themselves around their victims and pull them open using the suckers on their arms. Then they push their stomachs out through their mouths and eat the shellfish's meat.

 Stick a starfish here.

 Draw some more.

Sea urchins look like chestnuts.

Sea urchins are spiny balls. They don't have eyes or a brain, but they do have a little mouth with five very pointy teeth. They rub their spines on rocks to dig nests where they can hide. They also hide by covering themselves with pieces of seaweed, shells, and pebbles.

Hide the sea urchin under some seaweed and seashells.

Treasures washed up from the sea.

The waves leave a vast number of treasures lying on the beach. Walking along the shore, you can find crab shells, cuttlebones, empty shells, bird feathers, all kinds of seaweed, pieces of driftwood carved by the sea, and pieces of beach glass polished by the sand.

*Decorate the fish.
Find a shell and put it on the head to give it a nose.*

Seaweeds are plants that live in the ocean.

Seaweeds don't have leaves, flowers, or roots. Some of them anchor themselves to rocks or seashells with holdfasts. Others have little floats to keep them standing upright at the surface of the water. When they wash up on the beach, they become "beach drift."

Color the seaweeds red, brown, or green. Draw some more.

Hermit crabs change homes often.

Hermit crabs make their homes in abandoned seashells to protect their soft bellies. When they outgrow their shells, they move into bigger ones. They clean their shells carefully before moving in, and they block the entrance with their left, bigger claw to keep from being disturbed.

Hurry up and find shells for the hermit crabs that need one! Be quick about it or the seagulls will eat them.

Gobies like shallow water.

When the tide goes out, it leaves little fish called gobies behind in tidal pools of water. Their lower fins form a disc-shaped sucker to stick to rocks and keep the waves from carrying them away. They have eyes on top of their heads to watch out for birds.

Hide the goby by coloring it the same color as the rock. Add some shells and seaweeds.

Shrimp escape backward.

Prawns are big shrimp. They propel themselves backward with a flip of the tail to escape danger! They hide under seaweeds during the day and go out at night to find food. Prawns are transparent but turn pink when they're cooked.

Help the prawns hide by sticking seaweeds over them.

Draw some more.

Herring gulls are the beaches' garbage collectors.

Herring gulls eat the scraps and dead fish the sea and fishermen cast away. They also eat mussels, which they drop from the air onto rocks to break their shells.

Color the gulls.

Cormorants are champion divers.

Cormorants dive under water to catch fish and bring them back to the surface. Then they toss the fish into the air and swallow them head first. When they've had their fill, they stand still with their wings spread out fully to dry out their feathers.

 Color all of the cormorant's feathers black and its beak yellow.

Who built this great castle?

This magnificent sand castle was built by children. It's too bad they didn't have time to finish it!

Finish the castle yourself. Decorate it with seaweeds and seashells.

Color the sea.

Test your knowledge!

People protect the dunes along the coast by:

☐ building houses.
☐ planting reeds.
☐ piling up pebbles.

Prawns are:

☐ shrimp.
☐ seaweed.
☐ seashells.

Limpets fasten themselves to rocks with:

☐ sticky slime.
☐ their feet.
☐ a claw.

Crabs move:

☐ sideways.
☐ backward.
☐ by zigzagging.

On the shore, the waves deposit:

☐ beach string.
☐ beach rope.
☐ beach drift.

Gobies have eyes:

☐ on their tail.
☐ under their fin.
☐ on top of their head.

Starfish:

☐ have two heads.
☐ don't have a head.
☐ have one head.

When gulls want to eat musssels:

☐ they swallow them whole.
☐ wait for them to open.
☐ break them on rocks.

Hermit crabs protect the entrance to their shells with:

☐ their big claw.
☐ seaweed.
☐ sand.

Turn your activity book upside down for the answers.

People plant reeds; crabs move sideways; starfish don't have heads; prawns are shrimp; waves deposit beach drift; gulls break the mussels on rocks; limpets fasten themselves to rocks with their feet; gobies have eyes on top of their head; hermit crabs protect their shells with their claw.